VENTR

JERROD E.

IC(L)E

BOHN

For information contact:
Unsolicited Press
Portland, Oregon
www.unsolicitedpress.com
orders@unsolicitedpress.com
619-354-8005

Cover Design: Kathryn Gerhardt
Editor: S.R. Stewart

ISBN: 978-1-956692-59-4

Thank you to the following journals, magazines and/or publications where the same or various versions of these poems first appeared: *alice blue review*, *Hello Poems (a chapbook featuring six Denver-area poets)*, *Inertia*, *eccolinguistics (an occasional poetry mailer from Delete Press)*, *Moria*, *Ottawa Arts Review*, *Calamus Journal*, and *Titmouse*

This book is dedicated to L, "The melt on our tongue first was flakes"

TABLE OF CONTENTS

ATRIA: PULSE

L

our landscape: I offer you
this catalogue of plants

yes some are carnivorous
ingesting fly-flesh like suns

others might choke
on raindrops or blossom

open in the small crescent
moon of your hand

VENTRIC(L)E: FOUNDATION

light on our impatiens
vased alongside knick-knacks
window-silled—

      too late for coffee & the whiskey-
      hour nears when I'll write
      lazy poetry & talk about what
      you read next week

I watched your fingers tap the table as if the wood-swirls made a dim
music & the lacquer needed reason to shine. There were chips in your
nail-polish where you'd bitten or maybe something like shadows under
the enamel. Your cuticles needed tending. Your nails weren't painted at
all

the tea cup's lip waits for kettle-warmth

      liquid song

even now the hot water's hiss
elongated, an elegant vowel

      you are to me

::

rising steam : moisture on glass

::

are you to me

I'll watch your hand go over the craters your fingernails created. This is how it will be. You told me you read my poem this coming Monday. I noticed that you file too much away. Your touch scarred like the marks scalding mugs will leave

we are

::

condensation : sublimation

rolling down the moonlit window

impatiens' dew-
vase tomorrows

CHAMBER ONE—VESSEL

VESSEL I: DRAIN TILE

I heard a faucet drip, this structure
called house: some timbers, shingles & pipes
the water through them an arterial form
of knowing

    we lie some nights
in bed & can't sleep because liquid on steel,
plumping collapsed, is just too loud
why I didn't move to the right
the bucket a little

    we've become
in our not silence comfortable, tapping
stifles our breathing & any utterances
that might pass for conversation
but not as petition

    we measure our wait
below ceiling's seep we laid & said

that wasn't an issue: above the bed
molding discolored

        plaster sags
our weight's measure

VESSEL II: FOOTING

we affix ourselves to certainties: the power
will fail when water boils & steam,
up from the kettle, will warm liquid in throat
lastly tongue

        I do not know when it will
return but let's sit in this darkness
wrapping its thin hands around us as yours
in mine, while I whisper I am & you
believe this doubled touch

           or maybe I felt
in the present will, even though I have no name
to give you, unseen

        there, willing

VESSEL III: FOUNDATION

let's arrange our writing rooms not beside
but by syntax, you see my poems
won't pay bills & your novels, well let's
leave the real transgressions
to me

        hunker down our winter cloisters
there is a rage of frost with designs on our steps
closed doors are naked
openness's invitations

        will you redress your letters'
leaves, denude my budding words,
we have limbed one another well

            in unlined corridors
synapse until we wake
in covered boxes dreamt
mute walls

VALVE: RED WINE

spring took leave in a warming
of water
            summer then an unmarked time
when sweat mistakes itself for other
moisture, the nourishing

fall makes its delicate impression
in this parable of thirst
                  famished leaf
won't sip because it knows love
is the consequence of a mouth
closed to so little rain

VESSEL IV: GIRDER

without knowing the distance
between house & home
we fell from one
slipped into the other & holed
ourselves under the floorboards
to creak distinction

house : use :: home :

ATRIA: PALPITATION

L

of my rib I have made you
a beautiful cage

floor scraps you perch over
are my joints' compost

because a knuckle is a poem or a wire
my throat a latch for your song

through adam's apple's bars
metered syllables of doors

VESSEL V: JOIST

under the roof's shingles
tarred over

hammered down
we placed a dream

AURICLE: CHAMBERING

both couched we speak of silent things

a clover's head sprouts a fifth leaf
we count blessings between cushions

      what we can't not do to one another
      is the potential expressed in the forefinger's
      ridged pressing, a counting

      of skin-glyphs
      moles' rigid impression

blanket heat, your bare shoulders

      my touch
      a lung

      I sink down quiet

even the wind envies your slight breath
opening somewhere a clenched bud

ATRIA: PLAQUE

L

in priorglow, two twigs merged:

what is piety you ask
o you who stayed up late

who let breath
bind in cold lacework

you ask
wind rattles

please leave could you
enfold a twig what is

never was home

VALVE: SALAD GREENS

vent-air touched on a lesser thing
shaking sprout in the hand-
made vase, a tacky tourist this city
stalled behind basement windows

you always spoke of growing our own
paradoxes so we'd always something
to untangle

this season of wind circulates
& if it doesn't I—

rooms rattle ceilings
we don't ever remember
sky, not being in

here the hallway opens, my love

wears a monogrammed shirt
& may never tire roaming
your eyes' foreign streets

AORTA: SYSTOLE

buzzing interrupts bed-silence: we have
commitments today despite new snow
warm cats & naked distractions, we
we must go

                 our alarm senses as much
it hates itself & the mirror too but only
a.m.'s which often come after
our first waking actions

                        I believe
those should always feel like that half-
imagined place which is so close
to being as a ghost

ATRIA: TACHYCARDIA

L

your hand closes like blossom
each finger a pardon or petal
pulling into palm-center
invitation to tips as bud
to butterfly, each knuckle
flaps, lands & draws
from source sap that radiates
back out & opens sweet
pollen burst, each falling
seep into my skin-
pore like sponge or frond
slant dripping balm
or anointing dew as offering
bodies' loaves, sweatwine
nectartongue limb-
caught crumbs inward
scatter, blooming

VENTRIC(L)E: STRAW

I refuse to stare at the sky because it reminds me that I can't not have faith. A cloud is a corridor between lover & loved. Looking up, I am compelled to believe that my body is an ark & will one day sink under a bright blue deluge. A cloud is a channel tuned to god

the berm stretched for what must have been miles
tangled grasses just off it

I kick a stray rock
cattle watch me from fields
mouths full of cud

a dragonfly or nothing
straddles the centerline

prairie-chicken from fencepost flown

A thunderhead boiled like drought-stricken earth until all its blackness oozed over the sky & the echo of its spreading forced me to gaze ahead, not up. There was no visible shelter. Cattle backed against barbed wire, some lacerating their flesh. Others like they knew forked language. A cloud. I stare at the sky because it demands my intention. Cloud is. I am still walking. I am rumbled but unafraid. A cloud is a conduit for speaking in tongues

call : cloud :: answer :

I heard this once before

the berm stretched

downpour swallowed up the miles
cloud-call & every static finger
answers like an earlobe

Comfort that the horizon is wash. I am reminded that every raindrop bears
the sun's weight & the earth's taste. With my mouth open, I can't not have
faith

the cattle are lowing & I wonder
what it is I forgot to know

a cloud-gift on tongue
looking up

lover

a cloud is a cloud is

loved

looking up
the berm

CHAMBER II—ARREST

ATRIA: ÆFIB

L

we lie naked

these uttered truths
protrude like your hip

bones I repeat
them on the hushed

mattress, my tongue

AORTA: FLATLINE

lingual leap made when we met & now
mind no longer rhythms but some linear extension

        thing : thing

        no longer psalm
        world-objects
extend via prose

another point where our feet depart

        another breakage

to reconstruct the world by pieces

*de*surrect

unsure in what jump to *x*-height
will song the unrhythmed iamb

a poem is a joint
I am unhinged

the linkage between
heaven & hand

between all corporeal in the fingernail's curve
unfolding palm

our knuckle gone missing

our knuckle popped out & broken
no term for shape

other than severance

CONTRACTION (VESSEL & VALVE)

i

all night I thought our commune
not inelegant like the gown
you once stepped out of, toenails
polished but chipping
one leg out from under sheets
our mutual stillness tuning sound
some static waves between
our bodies belching into garble
resembling dreamsong

ii

if I had to say I'd probably tell you—
the bed ruffle's dirty
pillows complain of our headiness

I see faces in ceiling paint
textured & streak

iii

always thought the sunless stillness
an inquietude like tumult
squawked by morning buzzards
circling an imagined abattoir

but this isn't what I want to tell you—

I meant to say this mattress remembers
your bony hips

every dim reflection

iv

I should say to you what my arms bare
your spine's rigid curvature
my hand unfolding the hummed distance
this subconscious leapt after our bodies
slacken & breath is a visible melody

morning wants for us to give it name

ATRIA: PULSE

L

our mask: I'd like you to wear
the one that gags you with a rubber ball

& this corset, these tassels & what I cinch
say stockings up over your legs

leather whips like sentences
etched in skin

unedited letters for your back
welt-bound book

all along exposed

scabs revisable until hardened
read then as glyph

AURICLE: STENT

door-nick some laceration
declaimed or tongue-cut, air-
swath the filthy exhale of course

open-mouth : respiration
                    ::
closed-throat : inhalation

but that wood-cut's real so splinters
gather between forefinger & thumb

blown into corner cobwebs

how it could stick there

antique drawer-edge slashed across the jamb
tired hands no polish, no push

  this bed's really the first
  in which we made love

  our shared breath like sawdust
  disgorged from pulp-wound

putty rolled into a ball where palm-
grit holds from each print & line

a language

     how we now cipher
     that etched scab

AURICLE: STITCH

what did we like yesterday lover
we may duplicate today & repeat
so our sacraments don't become stale
tomorrow but with more or less wine

how will it be that I touched you
what words that you would blush
because I don't want to leave knowing

cracks in my hands left you
reddened & rough

skin pressed to skin should always be
delicate as how we respire

what words I'll speak you thought
excess small talk over morning coffee
amounting to a little blur
smoke blown off our mug-tops

AORTA: DIASTOLE

would you describe the sun's taste as cracked
through blinds we keep closed this bright
oppressive sometimes

                                      we seek drizzle days
our lovemaking best to gutters' soundtracks
tires on wet asphalt

                                  our rolled shoulders retire

I gleaned a corner where my thumb covered
the light & that keeps us bed-ridden, too
much shadow, the walls also seem plain
featureless finger

                              how would you explain
form without form, this is a matter of dust
playing in split beams

                                  still atoms slow
tired as puddles despite their best
stirrings to grow

ATRIA: BRADYCARDIA

L

you step out of our shadow that wasn't
our shadow, the sun's blinking departure
beam-curl to undarked horizon

obstructed sight the only obstacle
our shadow maybe never objected

our vision the shade now drawing long
over what's no longer seen
last light's retreat the image

that shades every lit thing you stepped
out of this simple act of leaving

pale rays twinkling
what will be is & was left

your crescent foot's penumbral print

lengthens so too

our shadow

AORTA: FAULT LINE

reproved & unshriven—an empty guinea sack
       for wandering   penitent stars do their best
blinking eye & soul in the Marinas Trench

swallowed by some whale & jellyfish-stung
       porous sackcloth a sponge   water-
logged & buoyant under a wrenching sun

bark the chorus becalmed & catch a wave
       washed up an arid beach like *sorry I*
squawked & parting labia pull back

a-sea   cigarette & lipstick on shirt
       collar   *I am* daze & daze without song
unable to tell fissure from folded palm

BLOOD MEMORY: ÆSYSTOLE

of half-wet snows, you went away
this evening left behind
widowed footprints empty
spaces sometimes fullest
after all—
                    I will not chase
you down cracked, warming cement
to the room we spent so many
sheeted nights outside ourselves
liquid shadows evaporating mornings'
touchable glances—

                    our home
is a broken hearth I sit among
mislaid brick counting each remnant
burnings in the bread basket
my famished chest—

                    I send
hours of present moments' seed
dispersals through static air these last
being wind-lifted, hung

ATRIA: CLOT

L

you have fled, my voice
is hoarse from so much thinking

our walls are soundless wires
absorbing what words, what I

cannot write for you anymore
I can't not write for you

are rhythm-meter
sung & sole

VENTRIC(L)E: ARC

wasn't water in the pool
but your reflected toe-dips'
moonlight ripple
seismic in how it separates

I drank that puddle until there was none left. Tasted the moon &
became frenzied by it. Developed a lunar tick in how my eyebrow
twitched like a wave or circular disturbance of some cratered surface. I
drank that. Would have filled the hollow with resonances of my own
arid ambitions, falling skydust. Failing like the touch now offered to
your inner thigh or the exposed foot your shoes deny

even stars immerse themselves where you've stepped

no wetness only mud
dried between sand grains

only dirt hardened underneath
crescents of your dangled toes

I believe the moon can walk on water
& so too nearby flowers when light
swims over your retina

mirror : miracle

gentle lapping touch

Your step slides through & blurs the moon into a dozen sinking stars. I am now sick with liquid weight. My head bobs like a celestial body in descent. Each distinct drop itself a distant sun. Your act's density. I am now sick with cosmic wait. A toe submerged

moisture is

we would now waltz if there was
still surface

I drank that from
your arched foot's ridges

as though you've stepped over my lips
orbs refracted in saliva

moisture is mirror
allows miracle

refraction : reflection

The drank puddle unmoving except the revolving overhead, ebb below. My tongue holds a sun against your sole. This immersion's weight, a universe of wavelets propping you up. The glow of galaxies in my image lengthening as a riffle from your bent & lowered toe. In our wake, moons & meteors recast my thirst. Motionless mirror doubling your leg's lift. So too your heel press

:: moisture : miracle

CHAMBER III—VESSEL

VENTRIC(L)E: TWIG

screen or netting—whatever it was
separation & mosquitoes couldn't
penetrate except with leg-fibers

maybe tongue

I came to view cloud-paths as new formations & their sky-cut wakes.
Blue like canvas without portrait or an empty robe holding something
stepped out. You came open like nostril to air-petals. Particles visible
with each inhalation. Exhaled atoms & movement a-swirl or crystal or
perhaps thinged out of what wasn't. Made faces where billows. Gave
names

what's called becomes
what's seen & so
is song

I came too

aspens gave way to some expanse
bird-chatter mapped a clearing

breezesun

sung recede

felt faint of
what I will

our tent-gaze a buzz
tiny hairs thread through
overhead silence
drifting on still waves

a dead hymn

VALVE: RED MEAT

I'll cut against the grain just once to feel
resistance in sinew, gristle

will be too tough so I'll turn
to how the blade slices easy through even bone

we'll wonder at what I did say & know
desire was what I didn't

your mouth makes a perfect O always
clumsy to the forked morsel

desire in preponderance
lips' smacking silence

what I will say resonated because
that's why you knew & take me in

ATRIA: PLAQUE

L

home's fullness is a woven absence
skimming back disbelief

this last wrinkle left
a tensed muscle

a scar

even balanced steps sink

growing old I knew
it wasn't intentional

awaiting these
atrophied returns

ATRIA: FLUTTER

L

there is a full moon
in the water

still menagerie of stars

your toe-dip carves
wave to crescent

makes new craters

constellations
to chart

VESSEL VII: JOIST

a dust of light patterns the far wall—
what we think we see is just
          arrangements forced

the hearth in our house has bled itself
your lips' particles at play
thin blue in the afternoon sun
easy this rest to nothing never comes

VESSEL VIII: FLOORBOARD

come watch this cartoon
it is as daft as the gesture
hanging between us, a caption
spoken in a clattering of dinner-
ware, I put the twisted spoon
around your forearm, I wanted
to taste your freckle & figured
that's the closest I'd get to surviving
some impossible fall

VENTRIC(L)E: STEM

dandelion through cement
aspires to sunflower

head tilted like what might belong
what fissure upward roots might inspire

There were blossom-fields, none wild. A bud will bloom unless some
fracture. Some seizure like grasp, like thumbnail. This severance appeals
to wind & cloud but remains potential. Promise is the moment before
appearance of petal

stem push : leaf pull : bud

light seeps through concrete
shines like what is was all along

      breakage a cradle

          infant sprout
instant sprung

whiteout of seeds blown

Perceived closeness. A rose is a rose is a. Is a distinction between bulb & bulb, is a gradation between beauty & weed, is a container for sight or sore eyes. A rose behaves as a rose behaves. Sunflower acts in a disinterested way. & dandelions yearn for a ray's blessing

soil or stone won't affect outcome

there were blossom-fields

    bee : pistil, waiting

    where the pollen settles
    sameness, a nectar

    as sweet regardless
    nectar by name

VESSEL IX: BRIDGING

at night we complain
about the house's settling

but stillness too
is loud

ears anticipate
silent

floorboard stirrings

VESSEL X: FRAMING

people it seems hang portraits
to cover bare spots & make their walls
look more lived

                        an empty nail reminds
us of spaces we need to fill, manifest

fate of an unwanted protrusion
is to be pulled out or made functional—

to divine, we interpret our holes
as something

VESSEL XI: RAFTER

ceiling is a surrogate sky, a place to nest
you might say when we lie on our backs
& make shapes of plaster patterns, always
wanted to cradle you, milk flow above

your breaths are warming winter's
final fruits come to our tongues even here
enclosed in the sheets of our limbs

I will forever speak as if there is something
the town is hushed today
along rails a snowflake won't melt
boxcars will carry it far away

last dusk I saw whistles & light come
on in the roofs of our mouths, your body
a house of drifted stars, a tiny home

VALVE: BREAD

you really meant to abandon this
pink nightie, virgin pretend
I, too, am good at forgery
my elbow conceals a funny poem

deleted this mix we made love to
but not the echoes our grunts
grown into walls

last night's last supper

scraps' stench cilantro & lime
here's some compost I kissed
you too composed to let loose
strewn about the yard

VESSEL XII: DOORJAMB

half undressed you greet me because you want
to be seen as more than your skin
than your name that does not belong
to you, slant light

                                    pierces your negligee
please touch me as more than
flesh negligent of how separate
we are called

                         this thin afterglow
contains us like these bodies
we are homes of suns

                                   housing our kiss
neglect of who remembers as we lie
more needful of this trembled presence
than to know our nakedness is
to each one's own

VESSEL XIII: CROWN MOLDING

why don't you hold me you keep
slipping through my fingers as moon
grasps this night's passage & still
won't rein in sun

     lover, the hour
train whistles & hissing kettles our breath
tired of being comingled
contained in this resolute bed

       lover, the light
has come in, steam rises on streets
we can't see our mattress' many coils
wind toward kisses wired in our dreams

lover, the hand is an idle mystery
the head is carried away by solitary birds
you keep falling through my arms, lover
indentured flit open
     your eyes
then close

VESSEL XIV: INTERIOR FINISH

the vase said home the fern
said home the bookcase said
home the worn shoes said home
the sconces said the frames
mirror the said caulk putty the
nail hole said home was once
in the hollow of what
hung said here the hearth
say was lived in will
home say said it is homed
will said during our move
wasn't says home our are

ATRIA: ARHYTHM

L

our imagined postures slouch
over one another like how
your dress hangs subliminal
until you step in it

your flounced obliviousness then

our thighs bent & hemmed
stitched together like the negligee
negligent that you're no longer clothed

you as bare as spine

fingers' posturing the pose
held your back's vacancy
this gown seems

your absent arch
a mindful straightening

AURICLE: WOUND

gilt-rose lost its hue, now neutral
budding like grass's pre-
glitter dawn—

     dew is a look that bends
     a touch that sees
     mouthfeel brushparticle

        a beam

saw dusk illuminating your dark aspect
you are shadowmantra

     fireflies the glimmering
     proof of night

        halflight

     a shallowing of stars
     to weep with eye

     swallow : starling
     ::

swollen : stirring

unoccupied moon

thought of sun's shoulder blades
rosy arms tense & squat

here an unquiet song

this rooted world born of orbplay

ATRIA: MURMUR

L

let's play at not remembering
I don't the underwear you didn't
have on when you picked me up
that summer

dress concealed your
nothing I'm sure is what you
said it doesn't matter our nakedness
spoke fingers

tongues before I got careless
forgot this language we cast
out of flowers growing from

your sheets I'll remember we didn't
not do so to one another so much
better to recall these things

VALVE: STARCH

I am sure that when the stalk dries
earth cracks & fruit is ready
to be pulled

night air conceals petalfall
you & I alone in our otherwise bed

if I were a heavier circumstance
the mattress today

reveals a dent where another
imperfect fit my shoulder might have
slept measured by your head's

if circumstance were heavier I
would still be unready
sod clung to my legs

wet roots I scrubbed
even after

CHAMBER IV—BEAT

VENTRIC(L)E: WEFT (MORNING HAS BROKEN)

first-bird spoke
black-feather sermon
leaf-pulpit echo
dewy apse

the naked garden becomes aware
its own emptiness ashamed
morning's peeping

      cicadas fornicate
      weed-dappled lawn

God recreates each day out of night's darkness. The star strewn sky, god's eyelid. Twinkling like the dust out of which each day is formed. To recreate requires a necessary destruction. Dusk is a suspension between erosion & erasure. The moon, god's blinder eye, helps us forget the world's rending

what if we woke & called

      blackbird

another name

magpie : magpie

::

sparrow : godseye

garden in stasis until named

nothing's closer to living
than the cicadas'
orgasmic thrum

We tremble through the night not because of god's systematic destruction because god leaves things like ritual. We shudder when we see the first orb because we know we are forgetting what to call it. In dreams there are no names. We

our first waking sensation is of blood-rush

erection : first thing named
:: blackbird's psalm :

The hymn reminds us how to weave with our tongues. How to feel air's vibrations & call

adam all
all atom

garden wet when we walked by

sweet-sprung in completetion

erasing's elation
where feet pass

AORTA: REFIBRILLATION

we've come to view our walls
paint flaked & some spots mold

    a smudge, a vessel

blue-green your body a gallery of portraits
how did I not notice our exposures
covered up where other peoples' pictures hung

    that once-there photo
    your favorite among so many
    I am never in, can never be
    in you the sum of still-lifes

there wasn't a frame there wasn't
a nailed vestige of some smile
on vacation maybe an ex-lover
event we've never spoken

wood putty fills the holes
you stepped out

that unhappening

how did I not notice curves in the straightedge

air bubbles like letters
erased over a face
neither of us name

AORTA: RELAXATION (IAMB)

not face but face's
intention not indention
but hand not hand but glyph

left when your fingers pull away
pull toward not to word

our touch : our tongue

language lingers after mention
our distance not our distinction

worded gift brought to our throat
indentured to song

our difference a way toward melody

sameness harms harmony
not joined but multi-tuned

voice : unvoice

O multitudinous
        lover
leftover muted

our likeness our only divergence
worth singing of

AORTA: SKIPBEAT

your ornaments piled with nail
clippings pushed back each cuticle
hangs chewed

a flake of your platinum band
curled crescents end to end

    don't see me this way

    wordless hymn

the slough ours & dirt-hung hours
burrowing, yellow to the quick

      remind me please

    palm-press echo

these fibrous moons discarded
blown breath unfolded
gathered dust from touch

    word less eclipse

BLOOD MEMORY: ÆDIASTOLE

thin treads of you on the page
on the sole of my thumb running warm
lengths over ice, on my still-
mouth invoking a split-surface from where
emanates song

       be as it were contained, be as unto

veins on a leaf, veins in the ice
my lined hand communicates unlined
echoes that call you forth in thin
veins confined

       as if my voice were unto release

sheaves split a leaf held bare
threads to the ice-lip that called
cracks into the page where you sing
warm echoes

       be as unto the confided between

my many names for surfaces
streaked with blue parallels, your thumb's
pulse still treads to fracture

ATRIA: SYNCOPE

L

can I make dumb sentences sound like rain
conversing with your bare arms, languages
of tulips that hold their cadences
dying gusts of legible wind

for you I remain mute so that I
might speak the words rolling off your skin

hold them in my throat's dry spring
until the sand that is my tongue
becomes your shore

all that nourishes is a voice
your freckles' wetness alone a glossary
whose vastness is the sea, whose lexicon
echoes in sky-wave

CONTRACTION: VALVE & VESSEL

i

you are waiting out the fetished midnight
I am not sure but this is how I will
imagine you staring at the dead tips
of plants you couldn't keep watered
streets slither with the lucidity of drunken vipers
& still stalks are drooping winds
poisoned before each had a choice
to fall as scales through your screened window
deterred by your unwept face you did not
even shed one flesh

ii

last night some women serenaded raindrops
to me they were breastless & bloody
each wearing a face that you masked
every time you closed the bedroom door

your lips your eyes a motion's excuse

iii

here you are at the sand dunes & I feel
nothing, here you are dining with my family
this portrait already shrouds

I am palled & I will bear the casket
an Asiatic lily sprouted from there
promptly wilted, your name reads a story
here you are at the hot springs naked
projecting on me images of your mother
I am breaking bookshelves my promises outgrew
let's fill them with one more of your retreats
wormholes opened beneath moving boxes
sparrows scatter your bedroom wall

tomorrow some children paraded cattails
& we chose the one we'd never have

another shot another beer another poem

iv

there my shadow yells at you
he made of so much sun he
volatile to the tip of the glass

pouring champagne down your throat
New Year's light I will toast you
again I wake to watch another moon
eclipse itself & crawl into a black hole
left my accidental collisions meteors
how you ignore another tide

v

right now, a man strung of fingerpads
touches himself to sleep

right now, maybe razorburn in your sink

right now, the sky's aorta coagulates

intakes of air, right now
blown through a clogged vein
clouds no longer spelled in letters
tonight slurs its sight

vi

days to come are spoken grunts
noons themselves
are dumbing, deadening

drunk are listless
blurred our numb

VENTRIC(L)E: LIMB

to love is to lip the prayer
spoken first in blood-rush
push mumbled from ventricle
to fingertip love's language
whole body sung

      I came to think of you as a name
      & in that regret felt the wound gush
      as starlings from an untwined nest

      your name from tree-branch
      from plume & leave your name

If the pads on each of the five fingers are aligned, one can—I can—feel
the heartbeat emanate from the body's center & expand through every
limb & appendage at the same rate. One index finger throbs into the
other as the other does, a transfer of energies that trembles the tips like
a mouthed prayer. If I hold my hand to yours, the imagined synapse
renders me mute, needless of names

      tulip the prayer
      sin naps mute
      to call things

systole : pistil

::

diastole : stem

my mouth is a vein
tongue an aorta
heart's hymn I am
da-Dum da-Dum

to love is when the song
need no longer be sung

when I love you most
is when I forget your name

By holding the pressed palms between the eyes, the brain detects the heart's rhythm & becomes idea. What I write has already been thumped, in contraction thought, in atria drummed

absence makes present
whole abyss filled
wound scabbed
& on its path

to not remembering

sutra sutured
no difference between
blood   spring   psalm

your name falls away
my mouth trembles my eyes closed

to love is to lip what's first
unnamed in blood's circulation

I love you most when I am mute

body- pulse
minutest of song

ATRIA: PULSE

L

that snow we've envisioned is
really not there

melt you claim you've seen
run-off from gutters

but for you I wish I could
make-believe our drifted images

pretend the trickle that once was
is flakes blown

ABOUT THE AUTHOR

Jerrod E. Bohn has an MFA in poetry from Colorado State University. His work has appeared or is soon forthcoming in *Phoebe*, *The Montreal Review*, *alice blue*, *FRiGG*, *Cleaver*, *SPECS*, *Word For/Word*, *smoking glue gun*, *Watershed Review* and elsewhere.

Jerrod E. Bohn has written *Animal Histories* (debut collection) and *PULP: A Manifesto*, a lyrical full-length poetry book.

ABOUT THE PRESS

Unsolicited Press based out of Portland, Oregon and focuses on the works of the unsung and underrepresented. As a womxn-owned, all-volunteer small publisher that doesn't worry about profits as much as championing exceptional literature, we have the privilege of partnering with authors skirting the fringes of the lit world. We've worked with emerging and award-winning authors such as Shann Ray, Amy Shimshon-Santo, Brook Bhagat, Kris Amos, and John W. Bateman.

Learn more at unsolicitedpress.com. Find us on twitter and instagram.

www.ingramcontent.com/pod-product-compliance
Lightning Source LLC
Chambersburg PA
CBHW031440120626
46545CB00006B/2500